CW00644216

VISIONS FROM THE **UPSIDE DOWN**

STRANGER THINGS

artbook

VISIONS FROM THE **UPSIDE DOWN**

STRANGER THINGS

artbook

PRINTED IN
BLOOD

NYC / LA / PDX

C

CENTURY

PRODUCED BY
PRINTED IN BLOOD

CREATIVE DIRECTOR
JOHN J. HILL

DIRECTOR OF OPERATIONS
STEVE HOVEKE

MANAGING DIRECTOR
PHIL LAWRENCE

VISIT US AT
PRINTEDINBLOOD.COM
@PRINTEDINBLOOD
INFO@PRINTEDINBLOOD.COM

1 3 5 7 9 10 8 6 4 2

Century
20 Vauxhall Bridge Road
London SW1V 2SA

Century is part of the Penguin Random House group of companies
whose addresses can be found at global.penguinrandomhouse.com.

Penguin
Random House
UK

www.penguin.co.uk

A CIP catalogue record for this book is available from the British Library.

Hardback ISBN 9781529124439

Printed in China on acid-free paper

MIX
Paper from
responsible sources
FSC® C018179

Penguin Random House is committed to a
sustainable future for our business, our readers
and our planet. This book is made from Forest
Stewardship Council® certified paper.

You know, after watching several seasons of *Stranger Things,* one truly has to wonder:

Do the Duffer Bros. have the ability to time travel? Or, at the very least, access to a really good time machine?

Stepping into the world they've created must really be something special. We have a pretty solid understanding of the "magic" of film and television production, but they've gone and seemingly conjured a physical realm straight out of the mid-'80s. As someone who grew up in precisely that time frame (I was about Steve's age, at that time), everything just feels right. Not only the gadgets and cars, the brand names and logos of companies that no longer exist, but the home furnishings, the architecture, the whole *world*. Hence, the question.

The look and feel of the show are so strongly founded, it only helps to give even more solid footing to the nostalgia that grows from watching. Or from repeated viewings, for that matter. We re-viewed the show before we set out on this project so that our memory would be fresher for when we began to get artwork submissions. We wanted to make sure that if someone sent in a piece of artwork that didn't ring true, we would know right away.

When we sent out the invitations for artists to submit artwork for this project, we expected a strong response; however, we weren't prepared for the level of the emotional aspect of it. Hundreds of artists answered with an enthusiasm and perceived level of connection we don't normally see.

As has been the case with previous Printed In Blood artbook projects, our artists have once again outdone themselves both in content and quality. No note here can truly begin to thank our artists properly for their participation, for without them this book is just a good idea. While you flip through this volume and peruse the curated artwork before you, we hope that you will not only reconnect to your interest in the television show that has caused you to pick up this book, but that you will also be transported to alternate versions of that world. Versions that feel at once familiar and brand-new.

One of the many reasons we put together these projects is that we are art fans first and foremost. Now, our process has been realized and we anxiously await our artists' takes, their unique visions of the world we think we already know. We love to experience that feeling of seeing a new piece of art for the first time. It is, more often than not, an amazing, eye-opening experience. We're only too happy to invite you along to enjoy the trip.

NOVEMBER 6, 1983
HAWKINS, INDIANA

Welcome to **HAWKINS INDIANA**

PRIZES

Honest to Goodness **Indiana** Est. 1816

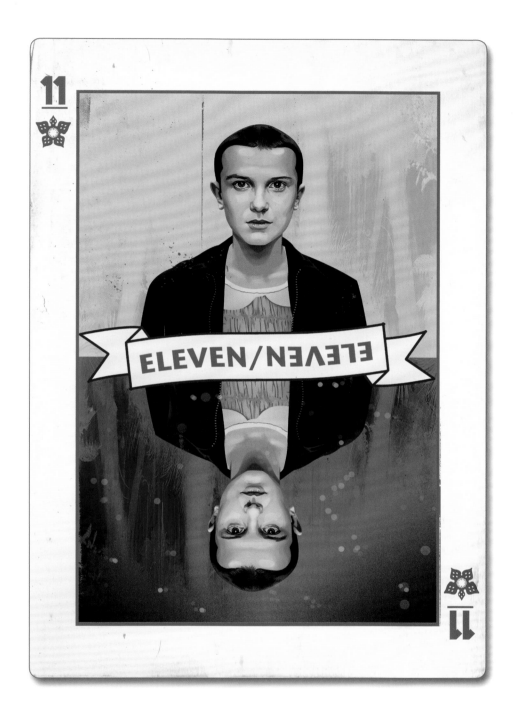

RICH DAVIES (left)

When *Stranger Things* suddenly appeared out of nowhere on Netflix in 2016, it felt like a breath of fresh air. Yes, it's nostalgic in its mid-'80s setting (something that appealed to me, being a kid of the '80s myself); but more importantly, it gets a lot right with its characters. The show's storylines are always told from the kids' viewpoint—which a lot of movies from the 1980s did well. In this day and age of the adult superheroes and their balancing of "grown-up" feelings and saving the world, here is a show that's focused on the kids and the way they see the world. Even the adults in the show are often seen from the kids' point of view. *Stranger Things* has often been compared to the likes of *The Goonies, E.T.,* and *It,* in terms of how it looks, but it's the writing that ensures the kids and their friendships are at the center of the show. I would have loved this show just as much at twelve as I do now in my forties!

BILL McCONKEY

WILLIAM O'NEILL

My childhood, back in nineteen eighty-something suburban New Jersey, was quiet and safe. However, underneath that pleasant veneer, just hidden from view, was a seemingly more mysterious world—a world of scary urban legends, fed by the pre-Internet kid grapevine. We whispered about the sister of a friend who claimed to see ghosts; a pentagram secretly scrawled by eight-year-olds onto the sidewalk at the park; the girl who one day just never showed up to class again; and that strange office complex nearby, where no one knew anyone who actually worked there.

Stranger Things reminds me of that youthful time of imagination and mystery. A time when a simple DO NOT ENTER sign meant a dark secret . . . just hidden from view.

ORLANDO AROCENA *(right)*

HAWKINS NATIONAL LABORATORY
U.S DEPARTMENT OF ENERGY

GUY STAUBER *(left)*

I'm sure, like most people, *Stranger Things* speaks to the '80s kid in me. It rekindles the magic of '80s cinema in an authentic way, right down to the title font. Lots of shows these days are looking to trade on nostalgia, but so few get it right . . . When I watch *Stranger Things,* I can smell the popcorn and feel that same anticipation and excitement that a trip to the cinema used to bring. I can dive back into the '80s, when everything seemed like a glorious adventure, and summers seemed to last forever. Not since *Stand by Me* has the adolescent experience been described in such vivid and evocative detail. If *E.T., The Goonies,* and *Gremlins* had an illegitimate child, they would call it *Stranger Things*.

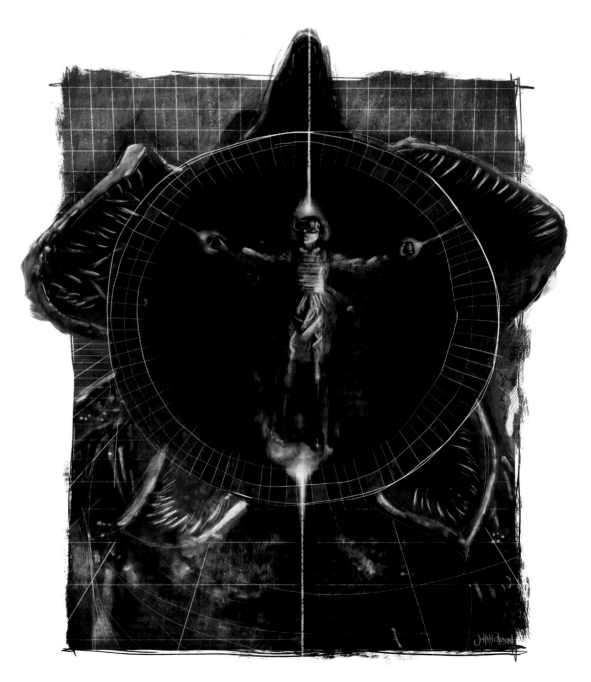

JOHN PEARSON

MIKE MAHLE (left)

AXEL MEDELLIN (above)

MATT MANLOVE

Stranger Things takes me right back to the 1980s. Being an '80s kid helps, of course, but it creates that nostalgic feeling so well, transporting you to a time when 8-bit video games and rushing around on bikes was all that was important. That is what makes this show so captivating. Returning you back to childhood, when your sense of adventure was so boundless. You really want to be part of these kids' "party." I always wished I had a bike as cool as the ones they have. My rusty BMX would have struggled to keep up.

DEVIN FRANCISCO (*right*)

MATT BUSCH *(above)*

CHRIS HITCHMAN *(right)*

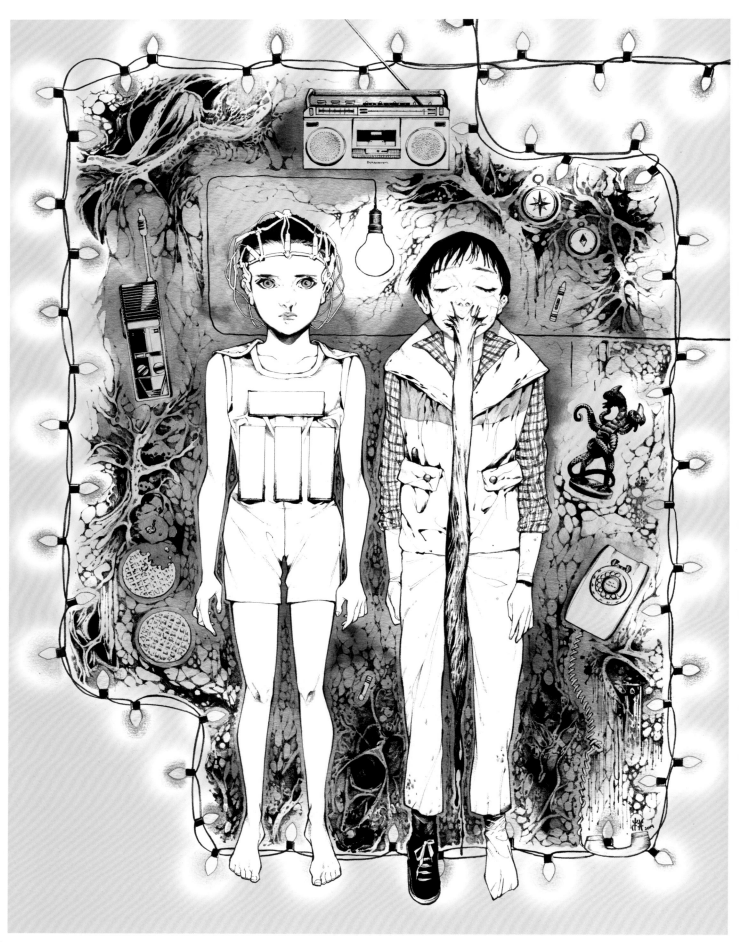

PEACH MOMOKO (left)

SCOTT McKAY (above)
I feel like *Stranger Things* speaks to the outcasts, nerds, and weirdos, and tells us to never stop being who we are. It's a strong coming-of-age message that spoke to me in adulthood, but reminded the awkward kid within me that it's okay to be unique.

ANGELINA BENEDETTI

In the Forests of Hawkins depicts the young Eleven in two different situations: The upper half shows her as a human experiment, sitting at a table in the Hawkins National Laboratory, dehumanized, with measuring tools attached to her head. The bottom half shows Eleven right after her escape. Autumn is foreshadowed by colorful leaves. Halloween approaches, and whereas the kids of Hawkins are looking forward to the festivities, Eleven is content with her waffles, breathing deeply for a minute and struggling to process what's going on. She's free at last, but not yet sure what to do with it.

MATT NEEDLE *(right)*

Stranger Things instantly drew me in, the second that I discovered it on Netflix and clicked on it. The throwback Stephen King/John Carpenter–esque vibes of the opening credits, the beautiful synth music—it filled me with pure nostalgia and reminded me of everything I loved growing up. Especially Amblin Entertainment. The show evoked *The Goonies* spirit mixed with '80s horror, with fantastic performances from the talented cast, and it's also well written and shot—it really was, and continues to be, the perfect package. I can't wait to see what future seasons have in store.

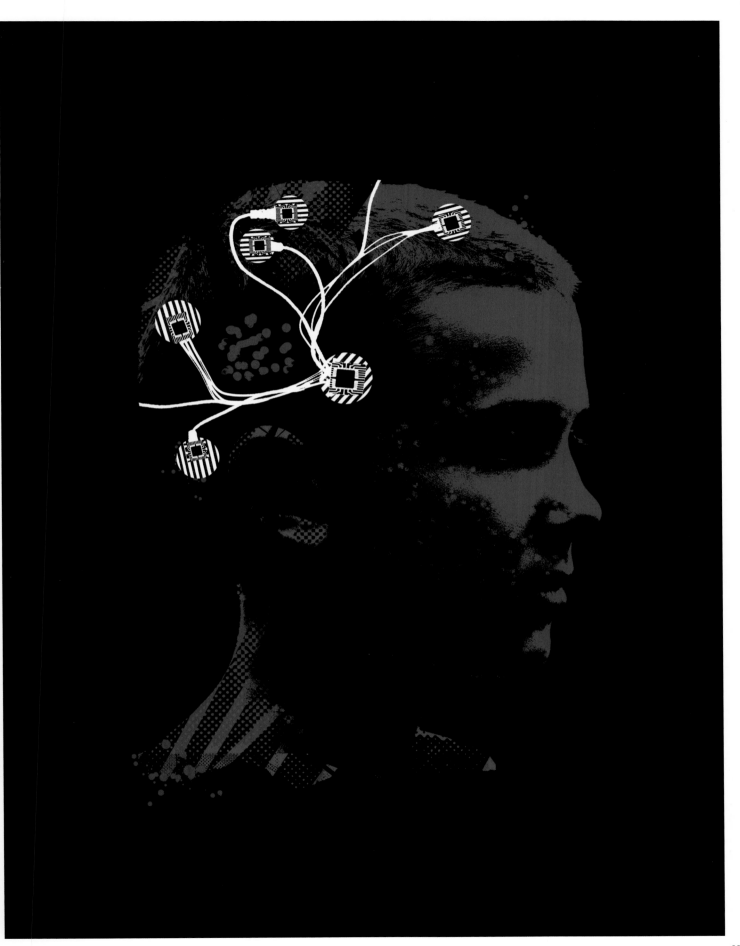

JOHN McCREA & DEE CUNNIFFE *(left)*

EILEEN STEINBACH *(above)*

02: "THE GATE... I OPENED IT. I'M THE MONSTER."

—*ELEVEN*

FARYN HUGHES *(left)*

What intrigued me so much about *Stranger Things* was the interconnectedness of the story and the believable characters. The series weaves together horror, comedy, and heart in a tapestry of nostalgic storytelling. There are no scenes that are unnecessary or gratuitous, for the sake of expanding the plot. Every relationship and individual storyline has a purpose that plays out in a crescendo at the end of each season. Despite having horror and sci-fi elements, the main focus is consistently the characters and their relationships.

The show shines a spotlight on society's outcasts and spends the time individually growing each character, grounding the storyline in the people. There are characters in *Stranger Things* that I have labeled a trope upon introduction, but who then completely surprise me with their story arcs. I find it refreshing to be so genuinely misled. Every character has a chance for redemption and audience empathy or disdain. This unique storytelling is both fantastical and delightfully human.

GLEN STONE

TED DASTICK (above)

MICHAEL VINCENT BRAMLEY (right)

MARK BELL *(left)*

CHRISTOPHER CHUCKRY *(above)*

ALEXANDER CHEREPANOV *(above)*

PAUL GATES *(left)*

Stranger Things is by far the most authentic and nostalgic piece of '80s-based filmmaking to hit the screens. Being an '80s kid myself, I was blown away by the level of detail and consideration that make this feel like a genuine classic— from the costumes and props, right down to the posters on the bedroom walls. I was taken back to my childhood in a way I haven't experienced with any other modern-day production. It had me wishing I still had my BMX, so I too could go hunting for monsters and on adventures with my mates.

BRUCE GERLACH (above)

BLAKE STEVENSON (right)

36

JAMES "BOARDINKER" DORMER SCHNEIDER *(left)*

DON ENGLAND *(above)*

MATTHEW DUNN *(left)*

ART GRAFUNKEL *(below)*

MATTHEW HARROWER

TOM KELLY *(right)*

Stranger Things speaks to me for a few reasons. First is because I was born in 1972, so I'm very much an '80s kid, and was eleven years old in 1983—for this reason the setting and time of *Stranger Things* reminds me of my childhood. The second reason is that I grew up in rural PA about five minutes from Scranton, so I played in the woods behind my house with my friends all the time. Much like the kids in *Stranger Things,* my friends and I spent tons of time exploring and playing in the woods with no parents around, so we had our own adventures and explorations. Third is, much like the kids in *Stranger Things,* I was not a "cool" kid—honestly, no one really ever is—but we were our own little group who were a bit awkward, and a bit too nerdy for our own good. These are some of the more personal things that keep me enjoying or rewatching *Stranger Things;* because I can see a lot of my friends and myself in the kids.

Another big reason I really enjoy *Stranger Things* is the look of the show from a visual artist's point of view. *Stranger Things* is full of so much cool eye-catching design and styling that you just want to draw all the cool stuff all the time. From the blue, dark nature of the Upside Down to the crazy '70s-style reds in the title text. Plus, the strange organic monsters in the Upside Down are so disturbing and fun to look at.

Finally, another big factor in why I enjoy *Stranger Things* is that it combines the horror styling of the '70s with the emerging superhero style of the late '80s. In many ways, Eleven is a government-created supersoldier, like out of a comic book, but she fights the crazy monsters that come from more of a '70s horror film background.

These are, for me, the main reasons why I love to watch and draw *Stranger Things*.

STEPHEN "DARKINKER" SAMPSON

44

03 : "WE NEVER WOULD'VE UPSET YOU IF WE KNEW YOU HAD SUPERPOWERS."

—DUSTIN

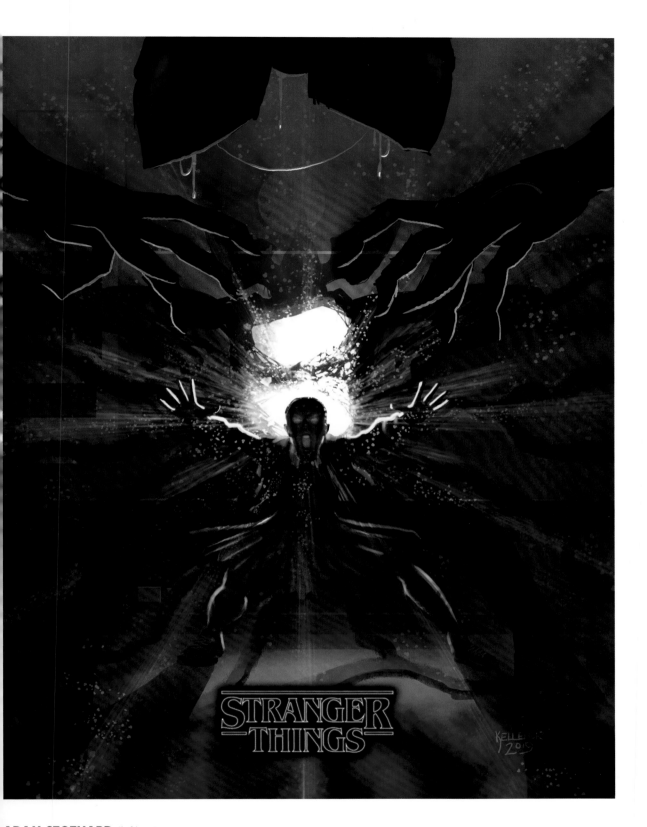

ADAM STOTHARD (left)

What makes *Stranger Things* stand apart? I think it's the meticulous attention to detail that's gone into re-creating an era very close to my heart. I was a child of the '80s and I love the subtle and not-so-subtle references to what, in my opinion, was a defining decade in pop culture.

MICHAEL KELLEHER (above)

CHRISTIAN NANNIPIERI *(left)*
There is a specific kind of cinema that blossomed in the '80s and followed me during my childhood. *E.T., The Goonies, Stand by Me*...They are just a few of the fantastic films where the main characters were children like me. Well, *Stranger Things* is a great homage to them all. Thanks to the Duffer Brothers, I can relive all the vibes I experienced watching those films.

JOSH CAMPBELL (PAYBACK PENGUIN)
Stranger Things is an evergreen story that continues to evolve and reveal more layers, not only with each episode but as you go back and rewatch an episode again and again. It plays with the genres of horror and adventure but evokes this sense of nostalgia—as if transporting you back in time to when you and your friends would hop on your bikes and find yourselves having amazing experiences. The story lines are engaging but the characters are the real heroes you root for. You can talk to anyone watching the show and they all identify with someone for their own reasons, but you get exactly why, and what they connect to.

50

JAIMIE FILER *(left)*

BRIAN SORIANO

Nostalgia is a prominent theme throughout *Stranger Things,* which brings me back to my younger days, from the music to classic tabletop and video games, and even the memories of childhood friendships long lost but not forgotten. But though nostalgia is the most well-known aesthetic of the show, it isn't what keeps me hooked in. What's interesting are the many characters, their web of connections to one another, and the struggles they face.

On the surface there's a coming-of-age story, where our young heroes make new friends, find love, and experience loss. There's a determined mother, frantically searching for her missing son, and a skeptical sheriff who slowly begins to unravel a bizarre and unfathomable truth. They're all connected to a horror from beyond. These characters are forced to confront unknowable dangers from another world, and, in doing so, they're able to grow and enrich each other's lives in the ordinary world.

NEIL DAVIES (below)

Obviously the story, the '80s setting, and the amazing theme tune are all part of why *Stranger Things* is so good, but for me it's the cast that really stands out. Everyone gives amazing performances—but you have to congratulate Millie Bobby Brown for making Eleven such a great character, especially in the first season when she had hardly any dialogue. Amazing!

RONNIE CROWTHER (right)

04: "MORNINGS ARE FOR COFFEE AND CONTEMPLATION."

—HOPPER

BOB DAHLSTROM *(above)*

JEMMA KLEIN *(right)*

STRANGER
THINGS

TONY HODGKINSON (below)

Childhood. Those films you were never supposed to watch when you were young, and the thrill of watching them anyway, either with your parents or not. *Gremlins, Jaws, Ghostbusters, Alien, The Thing, Aliens, A Nightmare on Elm Street, Friday the 13th, Halloween, RoboCop*, etc. I was way too young for them; I think it was naïveté on my parents' behalf, letting me watch them. But I did.

It's the same thrill and excitement I get to share with my own children, thirty years on, while watching *Stranger Things* with them. I am not so naïve as my parents in letting my children watch the types of films I watched as a child—and *Stranger Things* walks the fine line of maturity for them—but I know they love it as much as I do, and to me this is priceless.

DANE AULT (right)

Mornings are for Coffee & Contemplation

Don't you just hate it when your Morning Ritual is turned Upside Down?

Whether you're trying to fight off inter-dimensional monsters or just protecting your town's kids, we know you've got an important job to do. Start your day the Right way - with a nice, hot, Cup of Joe and a little quiet to think about the challenges ahead.

We think you deserve it. Don't you agree?

HAWKINS COFFEE

DAMIAN EDWARDSON *(left)*

GARRETT DIX *(above)*

L. JASON QUEEN *(left)*

Why does *Stranger Things* appeal to me? First, I am a child of the '80s. I grew up with all things great from the '80s. So a huge part of the appeal for me is the nostalgia—the lighting, the sets, the environments, the clothing, the hair; and of course the music is an instant draw for me. Second, I see myself and my group of friends—from my small town in southeastern Ohio—in the *Stranger Things* characters. I love how the characters each represent someone I've encountered in my past, whether they be my friends' parents or childhood friends themselves. Third, I love the story of *Stranger Things*. I grew up across the river from Point Pleasant, West Virginia, which is infamous for the Mothman. I remember, one of the first things I did after I got my driver's license was load up my group of friends in my beat-up Mazda 626 and go in search of the Mothman. So to see these characters get to fight creatures from another dimension echoes my desire to explore cryptids from the legend and lore of my early days. The writing and character development in this series is amazing, and flows so smoothly from independent character arcs to the main underlying story. I'm always enjoying the characters' journeys in *Stranger Things*. I love where the show has been, and can't wait to see where it goes. Bring on the Upside Down!

ADEM KAAN

BUTCHER BILLY *(next page)*

05: "I MAY BE A SHITTY BOYFRIEND, BUT IT TURNS OUT I'M ACTUALLY A PRETTY DAMN GOOD BABYSITTER."

—STEVE

LUCAS PEVERILL *(left)*

JASON DAVIES *(below)*

KATE CARLETON

I chose to draw Steve and the kids from Season 2 because I loved that relationship and bond of the characters. I remembered hating Steve from Season 1, and was shocked that he suddenly became my favorite character in Season 2—just with how much he evolved as a person. I can't wait to see how much the characters grow in Season 3.

ROBERTO DUQUE *(right)*

I never was allowed to go out much. My folks wanted me to stay in my yard instead of going on my bike to the neighborhood a few blocks away. Even then, my dad kept the lawn immaculate, so to run around there was a no-no. But, on rare occasions, my buddies and I could jump on our bikes and ride and not come back until the sun began to set. Or be out at night going trick-or-treating, and seeing all the creepy costumes in a new setting very foreign to my child eyes. *Stranger Things* is so special to me because the cast reminds me of those rare adventures with my friends when I was younger, how those friends are still in my life so many decades later, and also still have fond memories of those simpler times. We all see little versions of ourselves in these kids. Thankfully, the monsters that chased us were imaginary.

BRIAN "AEROSOUL" ALDRIDGE *(left)*

Stranger Things is a special show. It plucks on all the nostalgic strings for us '80s horror nerds. Carpenteresque synth score. Lovecraftian/*Alien* practical monster effects. Realistic Spielberg kids who play D&D and curse. It is the little show that could; despite the odds against it, the show prevails.

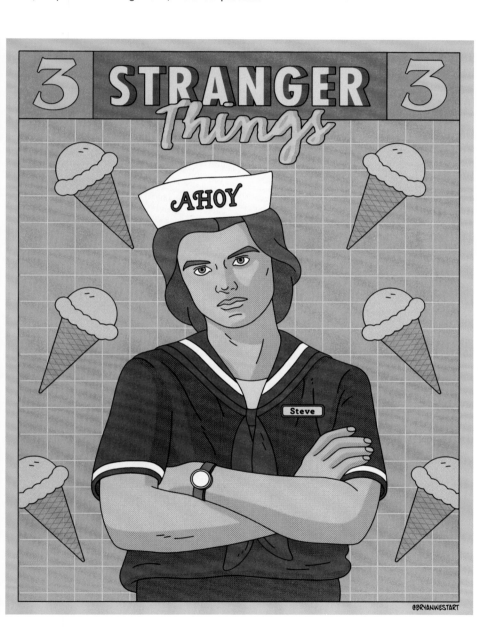

BRYAN WEST

Stranger Things is so steeped in nostalgia that it can be easy to overlook how truly original and well-made the show is. My love for all things shag-carpeted and '80s may have hooked me initially, but the nostalgia factor is more than a gimmick. Nostalgia is leveraged to remind the viewer how it really felt to be a kid. For the kids from Hawkins, every youthful milestone is new, exciting, and frequently terrifying. *Stranger Things* is equal parts wonder and terror . . . just like being a kid.

MARK BORGIONS

MATTHEW BRAZIER *(right)*
I love the first season of *Stranger Things:* the visuals, the music, the characters and their relationships. Although we see monsters, government conspiracies, and a strange Upside Down world, the thing that hooked me was the strong sense of family between characters. The way that Joyce, Hopper, Jonathan, Mike, Dustin, and Lucas refuse to give up on Will, even when others doubt their belief. I've chosen to depict my favorite scene from the show, where Jonathan, Nancy, and Steve confront their fears (in the shape of the Demogorgon) at the same time Joyce and Hopper are walking through the Upside Down version of the house. Visually striking—and the moment that Jonathan and Joyce feel each other's presence is particularly emotionally resonant.

CHRISTOPHER MAUL

The reason I love *Stranger Things* so much is its ability to take me back to when I was younger and life was a lot simpler. My dad passed away in 2004, so the show helps me think of a time when he was around, and the things we were doing during that time period.

KELLY MIGLIORI *(right)*

I've always had a love for the aesthetic of '80s horror, from the eerie synth soundtracks to the delightfully gross creature effects. *Stranger Things* captures all of that, but with the added slickness of modern-day cinematography. It's '80s horror that I can share with my friends who are tired of me making them sit through another obscure B movie. Where *Stranger Things* really excels for me, though, is with the characters. They're raw, they're real, and they evoke a different emotional reaction out of me almost every time they're onscreen.

DANIEL CAMPOS *(left)*

JUSTIN HARDER

As for why this show speaks to me, I'm sure it's similar with any number of folks that grew up in the '80s. I was born in 1980 and this show absolutely captures that nostalgia of the decade. The music, the tone, the warm feeling it gives me just watching it. The BMX bikes. Who didn't own one of those and go out exploring with their friends??! This show NAILS IT. We would ride around for hours into the woods and parks and do jumps and only come home via the dinner bell or dusk, never a text from a parent. Times were just different. And *Stranger Things* brings us back there . . . but adds a twist. And that supernatural element is brilliant and genius and this show is everything all of us never knew we wanted but now all of us need.

GMB CHOMICHUK *(next page)*

06: "I ALWAYS THOUGHT STUFF
LIKE THIS HAPPENED IN MOVIES
AND COMIC BOOKS."

—BOB

(left)

ADAM COCKERTON *(below)*

ANDREW SWAINSON *(left)*

MARK LEVY

I was seven at the start of the '80s. The summers were long and warm and spent riding around the parks and playing in the nearby woods, now a row of semidetached houses.

I watched *Ghostbusters* at the cinema three times in its first week. Soon after the release of *Return of the Jedi*, I attended an all-day screening of the whole *Star Wars* saga back-to-back, with only a ten-minute break between each episode. We would race across the road to the shop to buy more sweets. Seven hours of pure, sugar-hazed cinematic bliss.

Under the tree on my ninth Christmas sat a massive pile of *E.T.* merchandise. I still have a windup toy of Elliott riding his bike with E.T. in the basket. As a family, we loved Spielberg movies. But at night, when everyone else was in bed, I would sneakily put on the small portable TV in my room and watch *The Thing, Halloween,* or whatever film was showing on one of the four channels before all the broadcasts ended at around midnight. I would then spend the rest of the night too scared to fall asleep.

I loved reading Stephen King books, and Alan Dean Foster's novelizations of the most recent sci-fi movies. Luckily, this was the '80s; there were plenty of classics.

I would attempt to write "choose your own adventure" novels, but would only be a couple of pages in and already have my timeline tied up in knots.

My father repaired arcade machines, so our garage was like a small video arcade, with a steady carousel of classics like Galaxian, Rampage, and Gauntlet.

Thanks to *Star Wars, Carrie,* and *The Dead Zone,* I was convinced I would be able to move things with my mind and see the future if only I could concentrate hard enough.

What does *Strangers Things* mean to me? *Stranger Things* IS my childhood . . . minus the Demogorgons and Eggos; we didn't get those here in the U.K.

AKANE MORINISHI

Stranger Things reminds me of when I was a kid and monsters seemed to be on every street corner, in my overactive imagination. Friendship, first love, adventure—it's all in there!

DONNY GILLIES *(right)*

SANDRA KAMENZ *(left)*

Stranger Things just opens a door to my childhood and shows us friendship we all wish for. Full of trust, honesty, love, and adventures. It not only opens a new dimension of very cool, unseen horror, it also catches my heart with all the lovely sets, great actors, and outstanding music.

Let's fight the unknown till the very end.

JERRY MA *(above)*

CHRIS WILLDIG

NICK TAYLOR (right)

Stranger Things speaks directly to the thirteen-year-old me, always drawing, reading comics, or seeking out strange movies based on the VHS box-cover art. It represents a time when pop culture was all-pervading but not afraid to be weird or challenging to the imagination, but does so in a way that avoids being pure pastiche. Above all, it combines some of my favorite (stranger) things, the wonder of classic science fiction, Lovecraftian horror, and synthesizers!

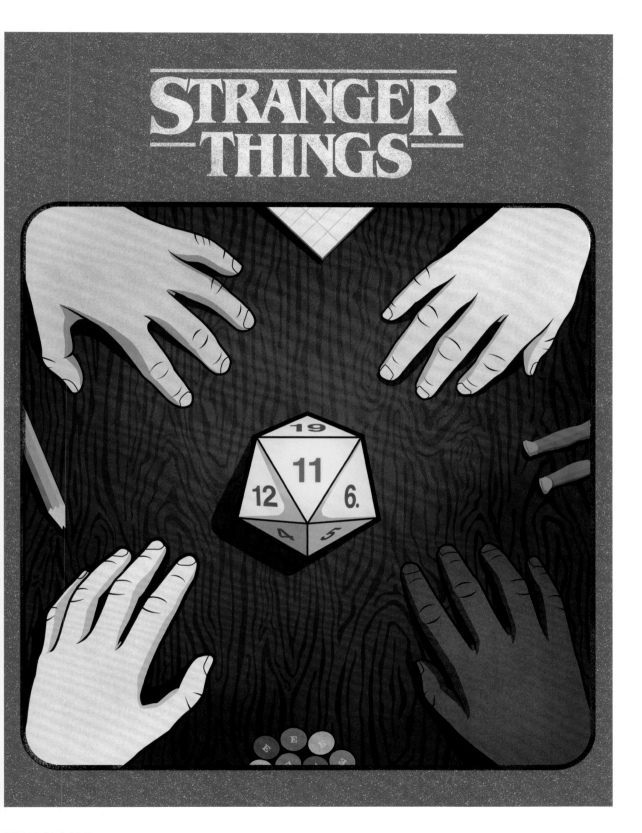

RYAN CROSBY *(left)*

JORDAN HART *(above)*

STEPHEN ANDRADE *(right)*

Having grown up in the '80s, I remember hanging out with my oddball, uncool friends. I remember hopping on my bike to go over to a buddy's house to play Dungeons & Dragons in the basement. And I remember knowing people like poor, doomed Barb—people who were solid, sensible, and kind, and deserved better than the mocking they received for not being part of the "cool" crowd. The creators, cast, artists, and technicians who bring *Stranger Things* to life obviously remember those times too (or, in the case of those too young to have lived through the Reagan era, have an appreciation for them). It's a strikingly honest and heartfelt flashback to that decade, deftly combined with horror, humor, and science fiction, with D&D, John Hughes movies, and Stephen King. All together, it makes *Stranger Things* incredibly unique and strangely wonderful.

Popular Scientific

PREVIEW
All-in-one GR-C1
camcorder

EXCLUSIVE
The Latest Developments
in Mind Control

We Visited Dr. Martin Brenner
in Hawkins, Indiana

Nuclear Waste:
How to Bury It?

The Latest in
Hand-Held Computers

Water-Base Paints

NOV 1983 $1.75

SCOTT SASLOW

STORIES OF THE WEIRD AND BIZARRE
STRANGER THINGS
JUNE
15¢
A Thrilling Science-Fantasy Serial!
The DEMON FROM THE UPSIDE-DOWN
by GUY A. TEESE

07: "SOMETHING'S COMING. SOMETHING HUNGRY FOR BLOOD. A SHADOW GROWS ON THE WALL BEHIND YOU, SWALLOWING YOU IN DARKNESS. IT IS ALMOST HERE."

—*MIKE*

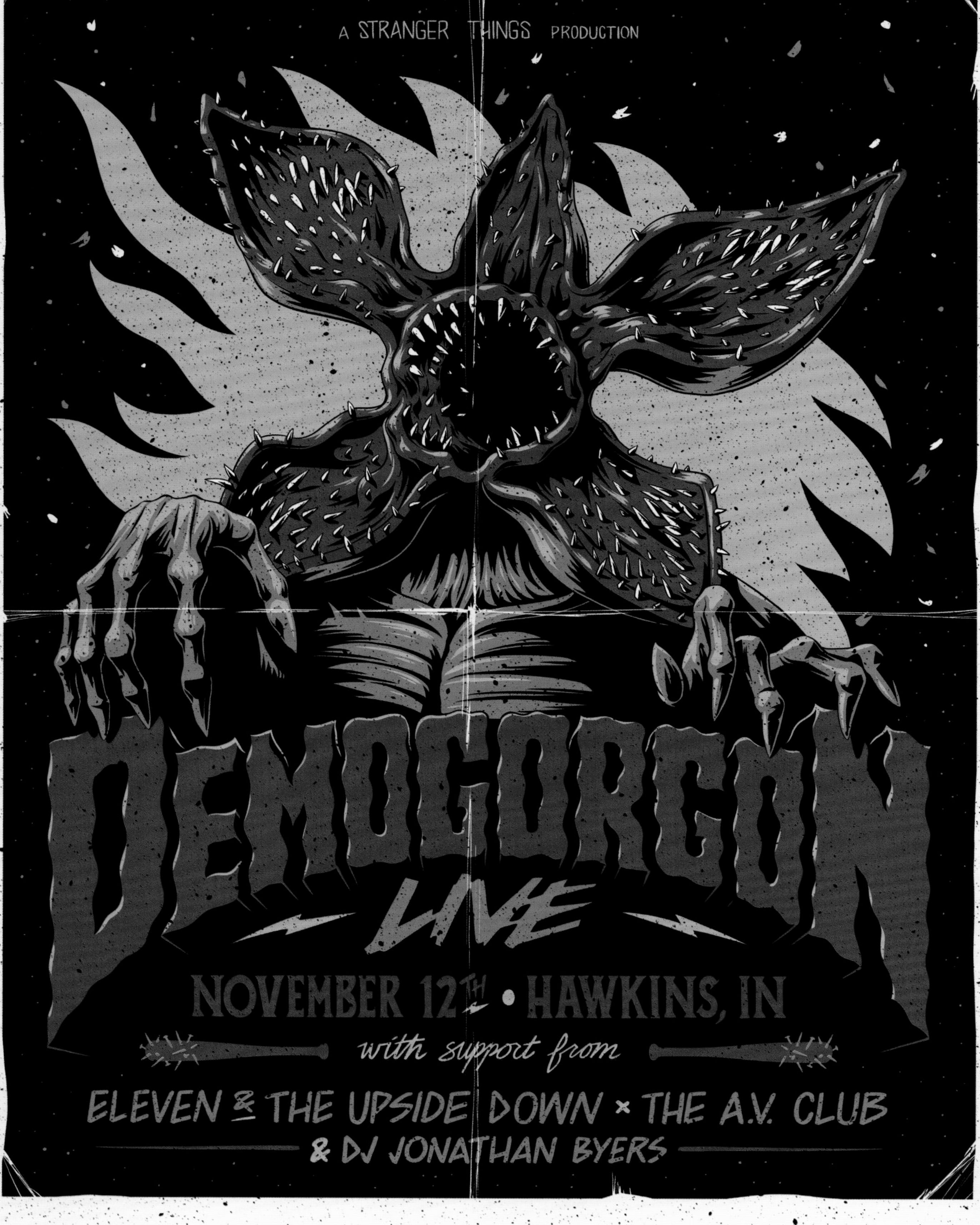
A STRANGER THINGS PRODUCTION
DEMOGORGON
LIVE
NOVEMBER 12TH • HAWKINS, IN
with support from
ELEVEN & THE UPSIDE DOWN × THE A.V. CLUB
& DJ JONATHAN BYERS

IAN JEPSON *(left)*

LUKE FRANCIS *(below)*

ALEX BONIWELL

Growing up in the '80s on a diet of VHS horror/sci-fi and fantasy, it was always going to be that *Stranger Things* would hit the right nostalgic buttons for me. From the film posters around the kids' bedrooms to the old-school D&D game, plus the many loving homages to my teenage movie-watching years—I can see *Stand by Me, E.T., The Thing, The Evil Dead, A Nightmare on Elm Street, Poltergeist,* and many more iconic films being given the cheeky nod and wink during many an episode. But *Stranger Things* isn't just about reinventing the glory days of VHS; there is a genuine freshness in how a horror/sci-fi/fantasy TV show can be made. Sure, I can nerd out at all the references all day long, but it's the characters and situations binding the story together that really give *Stranger Things* the edge over many other shows. Looking forward to more references and more seasons.

PAUL CREMIN *(right)*

Stranger Things immediately caught my attention and captured my imagination. Right at the start, the four main characters are playing Dungeons & Dragons, a game I spent much of my own childhood playing with friends. It was to this facet of the program I decided to dedicate my piece. My submission for this book, *Demogorgon—Past & Present,* is a showcase of the old, classic Demogorgon monster and the new, modern *Stranger Things* version. I wanted to depict the new version of the monster standing below the mighty, old, and largely forgotten mythical creature to which it owes its very existence.

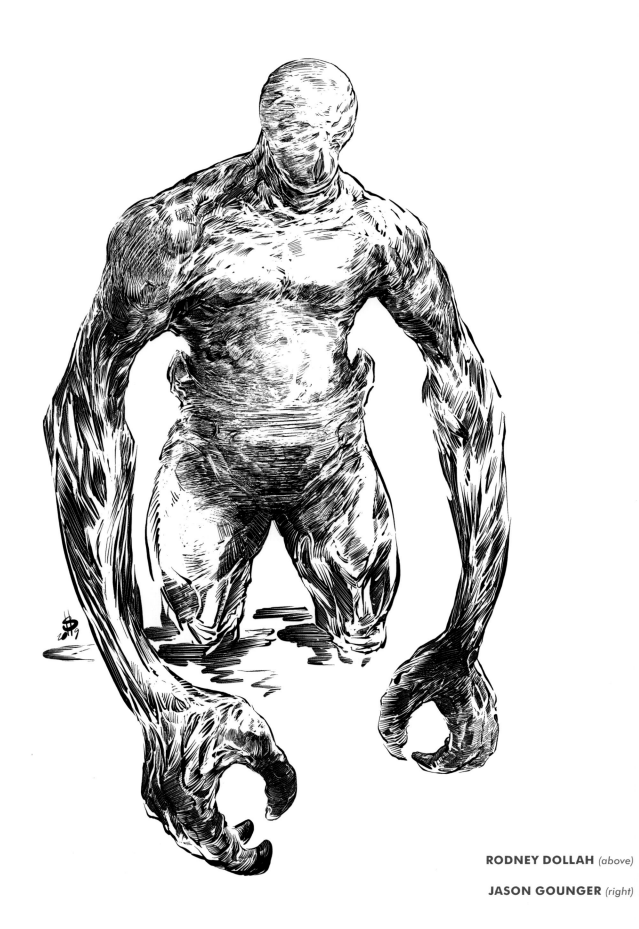

RODNEY DOLLAH (above)

JASON GOUNGER (right)

JARED (CIRCUSBEAR) FLORES

VALERIE SAVARIE *(right)*
I was a young teen living in the Midwest in the 1980s. There is so much nostalgia linked to *Stranger Things*—not just in the time and place it is set, but in the actors as well. I also remember a general fear of kidnapping (child disappearance, e.g., Will) in my community. Science fiction was big (but really, when has it not been?). The show transports me back to those years, when everything was new and intense.

MURUGIAH *(left)*

Stranger Things speaks to me in so many ways—the heartwarming characters, the nostalgic vibes—but what speaks to me most is the world of the Upside Down. This surreal alternate dimension, parallel to the human world in the show, is mind-blowing—and partly inspired by Ridley Scott's *Alien* and James Cameron's *Aliens,* two films that are a massive inspiration to me. The murky textures and tones brought out a fear and feeling in me that was exciting; I watch those scenes through my fingers most of the time! This is why I chose to work in charcoal for my illustration. The material offers up those same qualities of the murky, surreal world of the Upside Down. I'm also in love with the characters of the Demogorgon family, including the Demodogs from Season 2. The naturalistic, flower-headed, familiar yet creepy creatures speak to my surrealist sensibilities and art practice—hence the direction I decided to go in with my piece.

JON HUNT

SAM MAYLE
The whole show is a huge nostalgia trip for me. I grew up watching and being amazed by classic '80s films, from *Alien* to *The Goonies* and everything in between. So *Stranger Things* really takes me back to that time, as it captures the retro aesthetic and excitement perfectly!

BLACKOUT BROTHER (right)

MIGUEL (MIKE) DIAZ

TRENT BRIAN WESTBROOK *(right)*
Stranger Things isn't just a wonderful television show that pays homage to the '80s, it's also a cathartic look into the Carl Jung theme of the "shadow" of our own identity, all the things we fear and hate inside of ourselves as we long to be better individuals in this world—all perfectly portrayed by the character Eleven.

WAYNE TULLY *(left)*

CLINTON YEAGER *(above)*

Stranger Things has been a blast from the past. From Eggo waffles and *Ghostbusters* to wall phones and flattops. It reminds me of a simpler time, when life was all about cruising down the neighborhood street on a banana-seat, tassel-flying bike and wondering what D&D character my friend would come up with next. I've been secretly hoping that soon they will break out *G.I. Joe* and *Madballs,* maybe some GPK and *ThunderCats*. No matter what, I'm in love with this show and the characters. Dustin is a crowd favorite, I'm sure. But my favorite character is Lucas. He's got a little attitude, just enough to let you know he means business. I can't wait for future seasons!

SCAR STUDIO (above)

ALDO REQUENA (right)

ANGEL TRANCÓN (below and right)

One of the things that drew me into the *Stranger Things* universe is how it recovers the style of the '80s in its creatures and monsters. The Demogorgon is a mixture of a thousand elements that refer back to the '80s, such as the thin and terrifying aspect of the Xenomorph of *Alien*, the horror of *The Thing*, and the strange mouth shaped like petals that remind us of Audrey II in *Little Shop of Horrors*.

All these things combine to return us to that magical decade of horror and action cinema.

ROB STANLEY *(left)*

JUSTIN STEWART

To me, *Stranger Things* captures an entertaining balance—it gave me that feeling of the familiar yet kept me wondering and theorizing the whole time on where it was gonna go. I could see and feel the homages the filmmakers were going for, so the vibe was right, but I was completely riveted because the story was original enough that it hooked me and kept me there throughout. Also, I was born in 1977 and lived my first decade and a half as a suburban neighborhood kid, so *Stranger Things* hits me right in those nostalgic pressure points that are forever part of me. I know what it's like being there; being in that era. Those kids are like me and my friends, so from the first episode, I watched the series through wistful eyes.

GARY PULLIN *(next page)*

08: "FRIENDS DON'T LIE."

—LUCAS

ANTHONY GALATIS *(left)*

XURXO PENALTA *(above)*
It's a forty-year-old dream come true: What if *The Goonies, Explorers,* or *E.T.* went on for many more hours beyond the film release and for multiple years, with the same amazing kids running endless adventures? That's *Stranger Things,* and more. I sit in awe of each new episode.

SIMON DELART (left)

MATT BUSCH (above)

MATT BUSCH

MATTHEW LINEHAM *(right)*

Stranger Things puts together every single piece of '80s culture that I'm obsessed with, throws them into a giant pot, and creates an entirely new piece of pop culture for a new generation. The show is really underscored perfectly, with some of my favorite music from that time period. I hope that younger kids hear the soundtrack, look up some of the bands, and maybe dive into their albums. It's a pure joy to hear the music and see my favorite '80s influencers coming back in a new way.

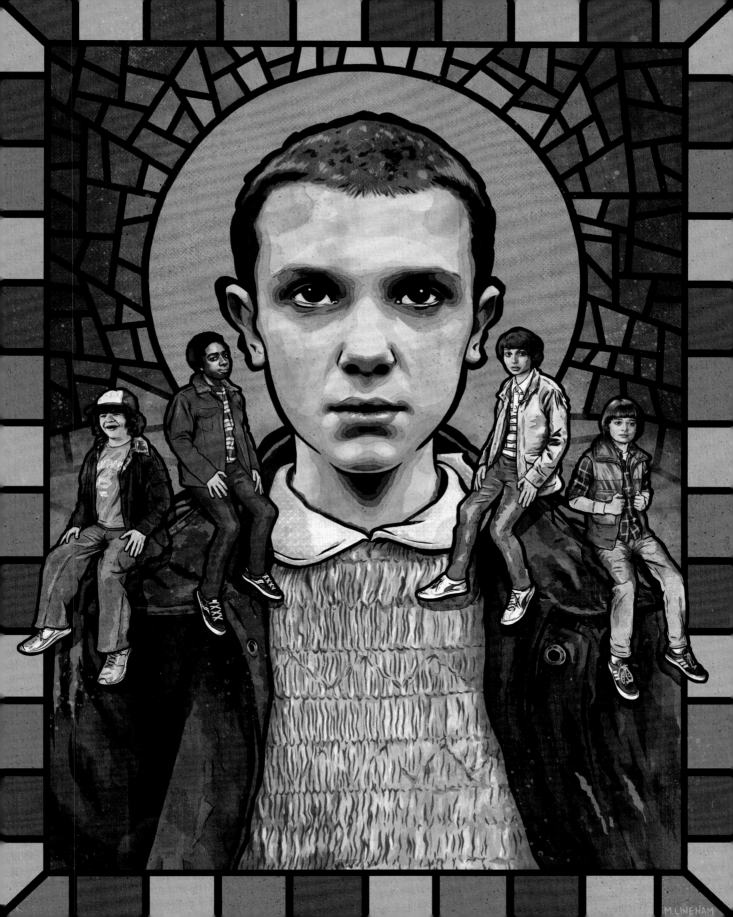

M.LINEHAM

REYNALDO PAEZ

The second I saw the very first episode of *Stranger Things,* I knew I was all in. I love the pacing of the whole show. Nowadays, everyone wants instant gratification and all the goods all at once. Well, this show gives you just enough to keep you coming back episode after episode! Oh, and the whole '80s vibe is a big plus for me! Overall, one of my favorite shows of all time!

DAVE PRYOR (left)

I really connected with the fact that these kids played Dungeons & Dragons in *Stranger Things*. I couldn't afford the game as a kid, but, not to be left out of the fun, I made my own by copying a borrowed *Monster Manual,* page by page. I followed that up by making up loads of adventures. A ton of work that took my entire summer break, but my love of D&D pushed me to draw and create. My friends would spend countless hours playing my homemade D&D as they navigated the dangerous journeys I thought up!

To celebrate the show and these great memories, I created an image of all the kids playing the game—which has the Demogorgon himself pulling the strings as the Dungeon Master!

SIMON HEARD *(right)*

Stranger Things is such a great series in many ways, from the various nostalgia nods to its in-depth attention to the details of the story; it has something for everyone. What I really love about it is how it taps into my inner nerd and makes me feel what it was like to be a kid growing up in the '80s era. I also think, in one way or another, it emphasizes that it's okay to be perceived as a bit weird or different, and goes all-out to embrace the hero within each particular character!

LINZY BUSCH

What I love and connect with on the show is that it highlights the fact that everyone has an inner hero/heroine . . . No matter your age, gender, or ethnicity we all have the ability to be brave and strong and stand up to any forces coming against us. The love and camaraderie these characters have for one another is truly one of a kind and that's what makes *Stranger Things* so special!

MATTHEW WOODS *(left)*

In the past I have made fun of friends for playing Dungeons & Dragons. It was a gentle teasing, but it still counts. I thought there were some things just too geeky to be cool, that there had to be a line somewhere. After watching the first season of *Stranger Things,* I became secretly intrigued by the game. The camaraderie between the boys while they played warmed my heart. I did some research and found that this nerdy tabletop role-playing game I had initially brushed off seemed totally up my alley. I owed some apologies. When friends approached me about starting a D&D campaign with them, I jumped at the chance, launching headlong into my new favorite pastime. Much like the ragtag team of misfits in *Stranger Things,* our group has been on a continuing adventure, meeting biweekly with no sign of slowing down. The celebration of nerd culture and reverence for nostalgia is *Stranger Things*'s greatest strength.

DOUG LAROCCA

Why do I love *Stranger Things*? Simple. Other than being a well-written show with great characters and spooky monsters, it reminds me very much of my childhood (well, except for the spooky monster part). Having grown up as an '80s kid, I'm very familiar with oversized walkie-talkies, arguing about who gets to be Peter Venkman, and searching couch cushions for unclaimed quarters. The nostalgia is layered and so well crafted, without pandering to the audience. I really appreciate the time and effort the creators put into creating such a thoughtful homage to my wonder years.

RAFAEL ALVAREZ
I am an '80s kid, so *Stranger Things* takes me back to my childhood days where I gathered with friends, played video games, and rented VHS tapes of the latest monster movies. Among the countless references to classic flicks, I particularly enjoyed when Will gets wired to the Upside Down monster in Season 2 and becomes his "spy," with nobody knowing if he is telling the truth or actually following orders from the bad guys. It reminded me of horror classics like *Invasion of the Body Snatchers* or *The Thing,* so I decided to use that as the subject of my illustration—just way less scary.

JASON MILLER *(left)*
Being a child of the '80s myself, *Stranger Things* is everything I hold dear from my childhood right up until now. It carries within it my love of '80s nostalgia, its foundations are built on films I adore, such as *The Goonies* and *Monster Squad,* where the kids are the ones who know what's going on and have to save their world from impending disaster, whilst the adults don't seem to have a clue. Couple that with a score based on the synthwave masters, such as John Carpenter, and you were going to have a hard time keeping me away. This is all surface, though. The real thing that keeps me coming back for more is the amazing writing on the show and the incredible cast; they are the reason I wait with great anticipation for the next episode.

CHRIS KAY *(above)*

DYLAN RILEY *(left)*

CARLOS CABALEIRO (above)

SAM GILBEY (right)

142

CAROLYN CRAGGS

BONNIE BOZELL (right)

Stranger Things struck me as a turning point in our culture when I first watched it. I had felt like most movies and shows up until then had catered to Gen Xers and Baby Boomers in terms of nostalgia and appeal. *Stranger Things* was the first show I'd ever seen that was marketed toward my generation—the '80s babies. I was hooked immediately, not just because I'm in my mid-thirties, but because I am from the Midwest, and had a close group of friends growing up with whom I rode my bike incessantly, planned adventures, and at whose houses I stayed over for extended periods of time. This piece is entirely composed of portraits and objects, because I've found that that is what I typically remember as I get older . . . important people, and strange things.

145

ART GRAFUNKEL *(left)*

MARKEE SHADOWS

From the opening notes of the awesome synth soundtrack to the '80s vibes, I was instantly drawn into this fantastic show. *Stranger Things* has a talented, unforgettable cast of characters combined with terrifying monsters. It's like seeing your favorite movie from your childhood that you had forgotten existed. Familiar, yet new and exciting, the show's elements combined make a new sci-fi classic.

DARREN COBURN-JAMES (left)

JULIEN RICO JR.
Although I was born in the '90s, the '80s and movies of that time rocked my childhood. They made me love pop culture in general, and definitely led me to the job of graphic designer/illustrator I practice today. Thus, *Stranger Things* and its many references to the '80s have instantly echoed everything I love the most in terms of adventures. And putting forward a group of children as main characters, with first love, school, and family issues, etc., adds a sense of nostalgia that deeply touches me.

NOS4A2 DESIGN *(left)*

I was an '80s hand-me-down kid. Even though I only managed to experience the last two months of arguably the greatest decade ever, I grew up throughout the '90s with all of the movies and TV that inspired a generation of kids before me.

For these very reasons, two minutes into *Stranger Things*'s first season I was irrevocably sold. A creature lurking in the shadows, government experiments, a ragtag bunch of misfits, and that soundtrack! It felt as if I were watching Stephen King and Steven Spielberg make a baby, while a John Carpenter score played ominously in the background...and what's not to love about that, right?!

These kids were mirror images of me and my misfit buddies as kids, and this was the kind of adventure we'd always dreamed of while tearing around town on our bikes, reading comic books, or watching and rewatching the likes of *The Goonies* and *Gremlins* until the VHS tapes refused to play anymore!

I binged that entire season in one afternoon. I think I was probably late on a work deadline or some other boring adult stuff because of it, but screw it, I gained something way better! My inner child was sated, and I came away from the show feeling invigorated. That sense of adventure we all have as kids—the one we all seem to lose touch with as we get older, after the monotony of adult life gets in the way—felt temporarily renewed. And I owe *Stranger Things* Season 1 for that. It gave me something reeling and pure, a temporary connection to that geeky misfit of a twelve-year-old I once was (and, to *some* degree, *still* am), with all of the *Star Wars* references, *Goonies* quotes, and iconic theme tunes that fueled my imagination back then still intact.

And for that, I will be forever grateful!

Stranger Things is a love letter to everything cool about being a kid in the '80s, and this is my love letter to *Stranger Things*.

JON HUNT

ANGEL ONOFRE *(next page)*

09:"YOU SHOULDN'T LIKE THINGS BECAUSE PEOPLE TELL YOU YOU'RE SUPPOSED TO."

—JONATHAN

CHRIS MALBON *(left)*

That was my time, I lived those years, I wore a silly jumpsuit and stuck a vacuum on my back and went hunting for ghosts with my mates. Otherworldly dimensions, monsters, and telepathic teenagers aside (but all that's still very, *very* enjoyable), the way the show taps into that time so authentically makes me smile.

Demogorgonia Dentata

ALEJANDRO BLASI

JOSH KELLY

JOHN J. HILL (left)

Having grown up in the '80s, that decade's pop culture has had a very, very special place in my heart. *Stranger Things* truly warps you through time with its visceral, loving nostalgia. Nostalgia that's not shoehorned in, not goofy winks and elbows to the viewer . . . you're just *there* in the '80s. And what really does it for me is the music. John Carpenter's scores are the soundtrack to that era, as far as horror and sci-fi are concerned, so *Stranger Things*'s Carpenteresque theme drives it home from the very beginning. The booming synths set the stage perfectly and hint at what you know, as well as bring a fresh, contemporary slickness to the table. I catch myself smiling every single time I watch the intro. More, please.

DUG NATION *(above)*

GUISEPPE BALESTRA *(right)*

KWASI AMANKWAH *(left)*

MALCOLM FISHER *(right)*

NOAH BAILEY

FRANCISCO FLORES (right)

Stranger Things piqued my curiosity with its horror/sci-fi and 1980s blend. Being someone who grew up in the '80s, for me this show has been a great blast from the past. I can easily enjoy the show's references and nods to films like *The Goonies, Stand by Me, E.T.,* and *Star Wars.* Respect goes out to the cast and crew for bringing the '80s nostalgia while keeping the series fresh. My piece is based off of Will's drawing of Zombie Boy.

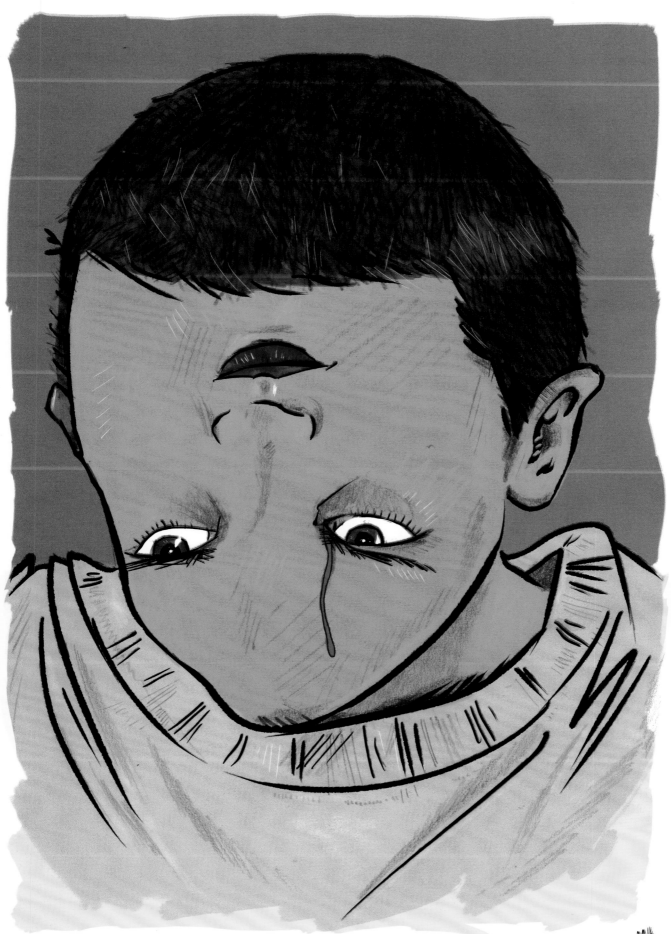

BASTIAN FAULK

Often adults forget what being a child, even a teenager, feels like. More specifically, they forget the terror and excitement of the unknown. The unknowns grow few and far between. It becomes harder to feel a sense of wonder and excitement in fear. *Stranger Things* gives that back. The wonder you forgot about lives in the eyes of a child staring at a dark empty space under the bed.

MATTHEW HIRONS (*right*)

Stranger Things is the best representation of the '80s I have ever seen on the modern screen. The style, the music, the environment—it's a gift to that generation, and allows us to relive all of our favorite sci-fi/adventure stories in one new tale.

ストレインジャー・ジングス

RIAN HUGHES (left)

Stranger Things puts me in mind me of sneaking in the back door of my local cinema to see *Mad Max, E.T.,* and so many other movies from my formative years. A perfect evocation of a very particular time and place in popular culture.

CHOGRIN (above)

RH STEWART *(left)*

THEORETICAL PART *(above)*

The *Stranger Things* series gives us these "false nostalgia" feelings; it contains
a lot of details conveying the indescribable atmosphere of those times, when
we were not even born yet—but we absolutely believe in everything on the
screen as if we were there.

KEVIN TIERNAN *(left)*
Sometimes on my long drives with coffee, I catch myself humming the theme from *Stranger Things*. That's one of the reasons the show is iconic—it has so many elements that stick with you. I loved the first season, and, as a huge fan of Halloween, I was hooked for Season 2.

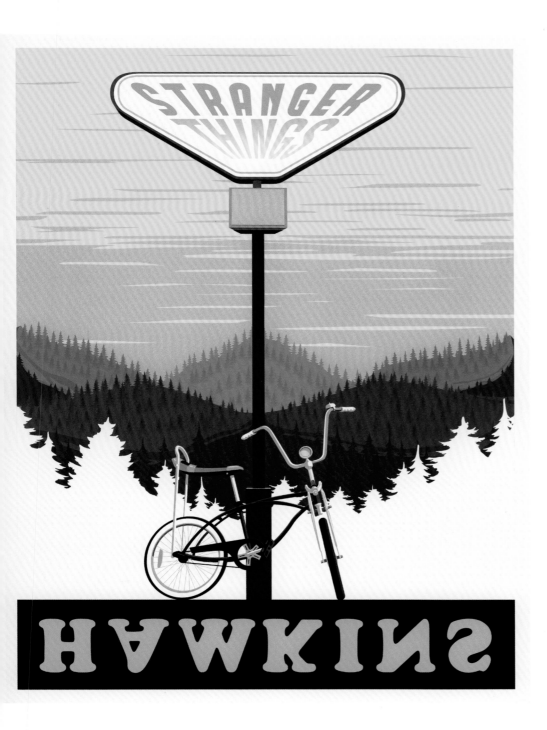

STEVE THOMAS *(above)*
I was born in 1974, so I grew up in the '80s with movies like *The Goonies* and *Explorers*. My friends and I rode our bikes everywhere. We wore backpacks. We hung out in basements. I can relate to these kids and the era the show's set in. It brings back all the memories. I also like the show because of the music and opening sequence. As an illustrator and graphic designer, I really appreciate the font created for the title. It takes me back to movies from Stephen King and John Carpenter, and immediately sets the tone for what we are about to see.

173

Inside the illustration:

MOVENS IMAGIN- EM RETE N RERUM ARC ANI HIJO & SON 1692 HAWKINS · IN ·

TOMAS HIJO (above)

CURIOUS ART GLASS (left)
What's not to love about *Stranger Things*?

The Internet has surely and not so slowly brought on the death of
mystique . . . *Stranger Things* returns us to a time of getting lost
if we wanted to, of having and keeping secrets, and—strangest
thing of all—connecting with our fellow human beings via body
language and eye contact.

Not to mention the inspiration to paint flies on pumpkin guts!

SANDRA KAMENZ

FELIX TINDALL (right)
This show is the ultimate homage to the time period it portrays. It encapsulates everything from '80s culture, and it does what it's set out to do so well. It remains one of my favorite shows to come out of Netflix.

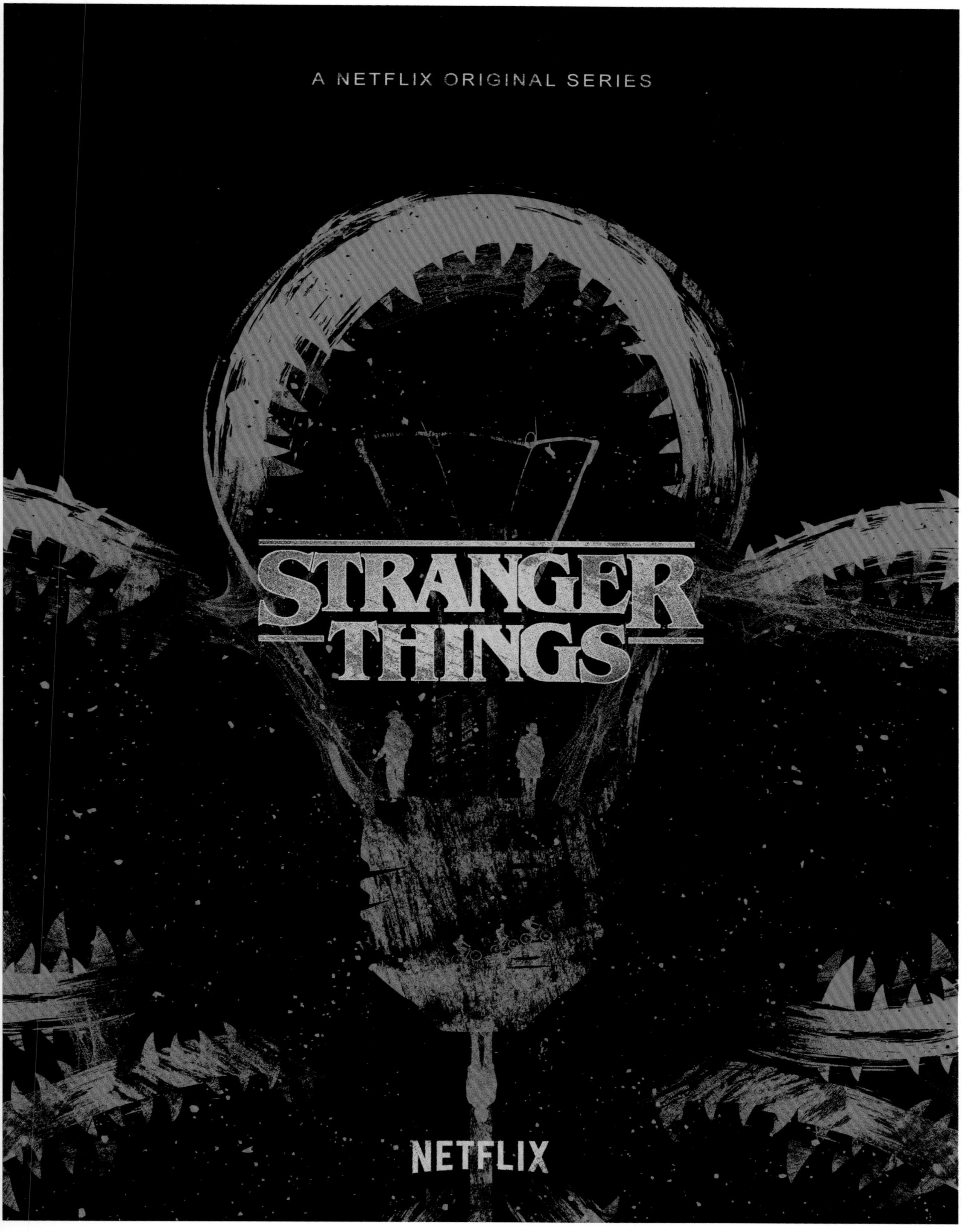
A NETFLIX ORIGINAL SERIES
STRANGER
THINGS
NETFLIX

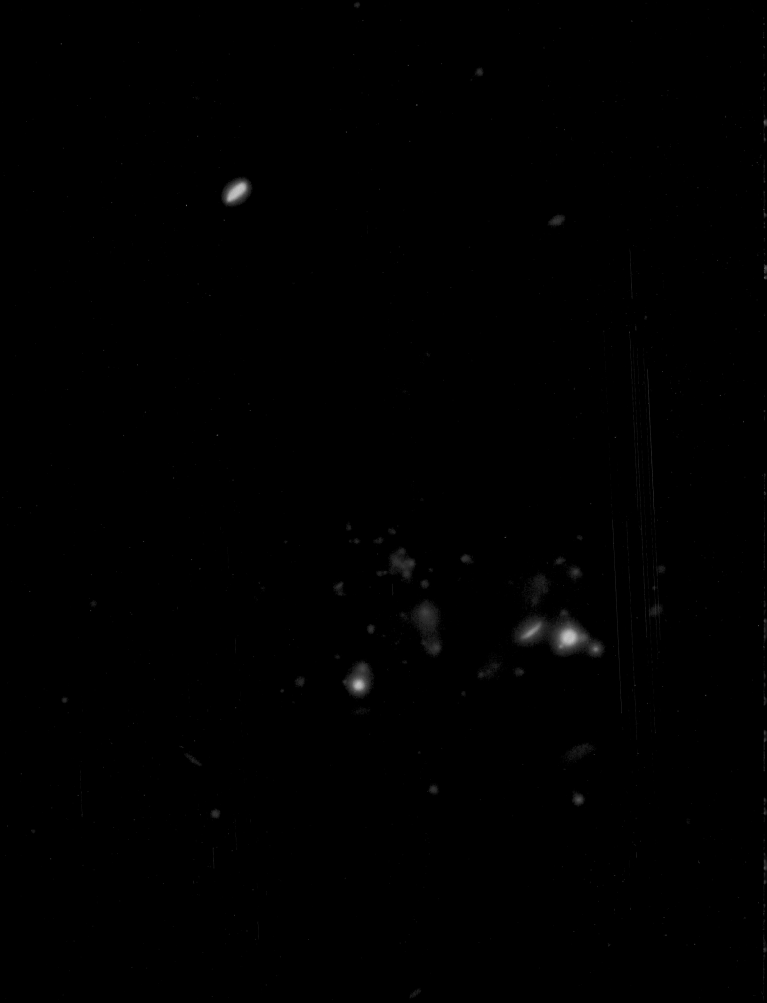

10:THE UPSIDE DOWN

NICK ALLSOP *(left)*

EDGAR ASCENSAO *(above)*

Our perception of the past can be diluted in the present. We are stuck in that very familiar emotion of common nostalgia. It seems like we're coming back to when we've been happy in the past. We are again young enough to climb trees, play Nintendo, and play in the street until nightfall. Our memories end up doing a full circle as the old ones merge with the new ones created by this remarkable series, with thrilling feelings in the middle. Stranger feelings? Not at all. The good feelings, the bad and scary ones. It's all part of the journey.

FREYA BETTS *(left)*

The series resonated with me because of the references to the consciousness. I love that Eleven was able to connect with the Upside Down via her mind and the sensory deprivation tank. I believe the mind is powerful (and underestimated) outside of the series, too. I also felt that maybe this kind of craziness/experiment may actually happen in this world, and there are certain things that we don't know about. It would be amazing and scary to think that there could be some kind of parallel universe, other dimension, or portal that has been opened—and we just don't know about it (yet!).

AARON BOLDUC *(above)*

BONNIE BOZELL (above)
This piece is simplistic in design, and leans on the horror elements of Season 2. Will is my favorite character. He endures so much through the first two seasons, and even though Eleven tends to steal the spotlight, Will's plight appealed to me more as a subject for an art piece.

RIO BURTON (left)
My husband and I are big fans of films such as *Alien* and *The Thing*. While watching *Stranger Things,* we both can see influences from such films, evoking a sense of nostalgia but with a new twist. The Duffer Brothers have done such a fantastic job of shaping their influences into a fresh story that keeps us on the edge of our seats and sends chills down our spines.

CHRISTA CASSANO (*above*)

BRYAN FYFFE (*right*)

MATT BUSCH

It shouldn't have worked. On paper, the genesis for *Stranger Things* just doesn't seem like it would resonate with today's audience. The '80s in general are a nostalgic conundrum, as anyone who lived them, *loved them*; and yet anyone who tries to channel the "big" decade usually falls into a sad cliché of what people think those years were like.

But that's a testament to the genius of the Duffer Brothers. On the surface, they have captured the true time period in a way that hasn't been seen before. *Stranger Things* somehow feels more '80s than the films that were released during those years. The props. The music. The lingo. The *wallpaper*!

Of course, their ingenuity in channeling that time period goes much deeper. Sure, homage is paid to some of the most iconic films of the '80s, but the brilliance goes even deeper than the plot. What the Duffer Brothers have managed to do, that I have yet to experience anywhere else, is capture the *magic* of the '80s. And that's where most filmmakers trying to do so fall flat. *Stranger Things* is filled with wonderment. It has all of the emotions you felt when seeing the fantastical films of that era.

So, for my take on *Stranger Things,* I wanted to do something a little different and try to capture those emotions. Discovery. Desperation. Terror. Determination. Compassion. All coming-of-age moments that are just magical. Friends bonding in a way that today's social media generation craves.

I'm ecstatic that this was a time I lived in as a young boy. What an incredible time to grow up! And now, thanks to *Stranger Things,* it's a time and a feeling I can share.

ALICE MEICHI LI (right)

SIMON CARPENTER (left)

Stranger Things gripped me from the start. The haunting title music and overall retro vibe put me right back there in the '80s. The show has such a nostalgic feel, but that isn't the only thing going for it. Great direction, story, production, and characters make it a must-watch for me. It has so many elements that resonate with me that it became a favorite show very quickly. I'm so looking forward to what they do with the characters next, and I hope the show carries on being as great as it has been so far.

JOE CORRONEY (above)

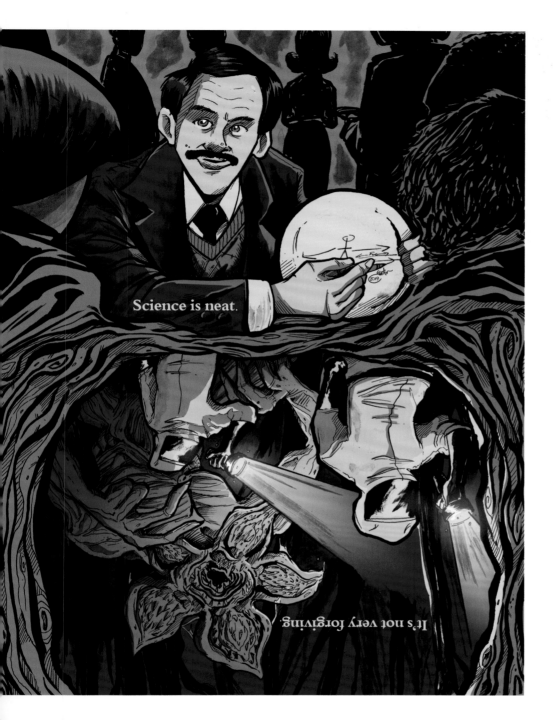

Science is neat.

It's not very forgiving

RYAN CASKEY (left)

"The Goonies and Stand by Me meets Lovecraft and Stephen King." That is how a friend convinced me to give Stranger Things a shot. Little did I know that I would be transported to another time and another place, but one that wasn't all that unfamiliar. The show reminded me of a simpler time spent riding bikes with friends in our neighborhood, exploring and letting our imaginations run wild. And while we were all Wills, Lucases, and Dustins, in our minds, we were Elevens.

JUSTIN CASTANEDA (above)

MARK STROUD

When *Stranger Things* came out, I didn't really know what to expect, as it was shrouded in mystery—but it had that '80s vibe, so I had to know more. Being a child in the '80s, I grew up with films like *The Goonies* and *Stand by Me,* and arcade machines, and so many of the things referenced in the show that it was like going back to that time. I love the look of the show, the cinematography and the music, it just captures the nostalgia perfectly—and the acting of the kids is really as good as any in the films I love from the past. To me, *Stranger Things* is more than a TV show. It's a look into what made an era of entertainment so great.

CODY VROSH *(right)*

I love the duality of fantasy worlds in *Stranger Things*. It encapsulates the childlike wonder of things we have yet to discover, juxtaposed with the true horror of things we can never understand. Like a lot of artists, I spend a good deal of time in fantasy worlds, at times leaving my grasp on reality a little tenuous. Joyce Byers really speaks to me specifically as the hero of the story. Trusting what she knows to be unbelievable, against those who think she's losing her mind, and fighting without doubt or hesitation for everything she holds dear in a world that no longer makes sense.

DUSTIN GOEBEL *(left)*

JULIE FORDHAM
One of the best parts about *Stranger Things* for me is that feeling of nostalgia I get watching the show. I was a child in the '80s so it definitely takes me back, and while it has all the qualities of something I've seen before, it's 100 percent new and exciting content.

JOEY REX *(above)*

BERNIE JEZOWSKI *(right)*

ROBERT JIMENEZ (left)

The opening scene in the first episode of *Stranger Things* hooked me immediately. Some people I know said they were really hooked after the second episode. But for me, the first scenes created a perfect sensory flashback of some of my favorite '80s films, and of playing Dungeons & Dragons with friends. That, along with the immediate likability of the kids and the ominous threat, was all I needed to keep watching. Eventually, all the episodes would go on to strike some nostalgic note. So, in creating my piece for the book, I was drawn to include a few of the elements that spoke to me from that time period: the mixtape and the D&D dice.

JOSHUA GREEN

IAN MacDOUGALL *(above)*

TOMASZ MAJEWSKI *(right)*

HEATHER LANDRY (above)

ANA KAHANA (left)
Stranger Things brings back the curiosity that I felt about life when I was growing up. Facing my biggest fears, and being brave enough to overcome all of them.

LUKE PARKER *(above)*

KRISTOPHER McCLANAHAN *(right)*

CHRIS CALLAHAN *(left)*

JERRY PESCE *(above)*
The moment I saw this amazing show on Netflix, I was floored by how many of my different loves were touched upon. I grew up loving monsters, and playing D&D all the time. The way *Stranger Things* connects all those nostalgic, cool, scary, and sci-fi movies I grew up on into one great show made me as excited to create this piece as I am to see the next season!

L. JASON QUEEN *(left)*

JUSTIN CURRIE

Growing up, I watched too many horror movies. This show felt like revisiting all those movies from my childhood that I probably shouldn't have been watching.

I still love going back to rewatch the classics, and that's almost what *Stranger Things* felt like to me, an amazing classic horror movie . . . that lasted eight hours.

ALEKSEY RICO *(next page)*

11: WHO IS JANE IVES?

SCOTT WOOLSTON (left)

SARAH ELKINS (above)

I was born in the mid '80s. Growing up, I probably watched more horror movies than I should have at an early age—but it worked out, since I write fantasy/horror stuff now. I really loved John Carpenter's *The Thing*, but also watched movies like *The Goonies* and *Flight of the Navigator*. When I first saw *Stranger Things*, I was hooked. It was a wonderful mix of weird 1980s coming-of-age stories and the sort of body horror and psychological horror I love. On top of the genres it mashes together, it is full of detailed, complex characters and interesting plots. I have been pleasantly surprised while watching because normally I can tell where a show or book will go storywise (this has been my curse for a long time—since before I started writing professionally). However, *Stranger Things* has been surprisingly fresh despite the use of the tropes I grew up with. It's also wonderful that the show is full of well-written female characters who have agency in their story lines. I look forward to what the show will do in the future.

SHEILA C.
There's a specific time in a person's life when they start to become very aware of pop culture through movies. For me, it was when I saw *E.T.* in the theater.

I grew up in the '80s, and the pop culture of the time vividly colored my childhood. I remember neighborhood kids playing Dungeons & Dragons, watching the "Thriller" music video over and over, and using my Pac-Man sleeping bag for sleepovers. I remember *Star Wars* action figures littering my friends' bedrooms. I played with my Atari 2600 and Transformers, and would ride my bike with my friends until the streetlights came on. I had a crush on Marty McFly.

It feels like I'm cracking open a time capsule whenever I watch *Stranger Things*. A wave of nostalgia washes over me, like I imagine it does for most people my age who also enjoy this show. The '80s were such a fantastic time to grow up. This show brings all that back in full force.

I love Eleven. I picked this scene because it illustrates the themes of protection, revenge, loyalty, and female empowerment. I love when this weird, lovable girl gets to feel powerful by helping and protecting her friend. Despite everything that's happened to her, she's still a great kid.

RICK (DIENZO) BLANCO *(right)*

LON CHAN *(left)*

Stranger Things is more than a TV series—
it brings together the best of my childhood
memories and some darker fears too, all
bound together with an amazing thematic
soundtrack. The characters make up a classic
team with each having their own special
part to play within the bigger adventure.
Every episode is its own short story—another
week's jaunt into this other world—but each
builds a new piece of the picture. I also love
the simpler technology, back in the days
when you could easily create an innovative
solution to a problem with just a walkie-
talkie, some tape, and a compass! It all feels
so much more hands-on and real than many
modern-day series and films.

My illustration is inspired by the duality that
runs throughout the whole show, the good
and bad, the real world and the Upside
Down, the children and adults, the jocks
and the nerds, all playing their part in one
incredible story. So I've created *Channel
Eleven* in a kind of duotone that, when first
viewed, gives an intriguing and captivating
mix, drawing the viewer in to catch parts of
the whole. But when viewed with 3-D specs
(the classic blue and red ones), each channel
shows its own distinct character.

VICTOR CASTRO, TAYLOR SHARPSTEN & ANWAR HANARO

221

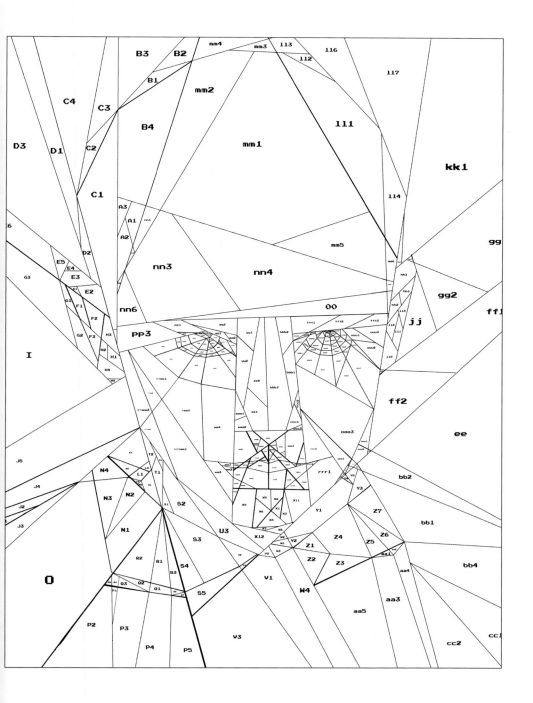

NICOLE FALK

About the art process: Paper piecing is a two-part technique in the world of quilting. First, the image is drawn and reversed. Each line represents a seam and is laid in such a way that they build off of a central point. Each geometric piece is then numbered. The paper is then used as a foundation, and fabric is overlapped as it is sewn directly onto the paper, allowing the paper to be removed when the piece is fully assembled.

JAMES HOBSON *(left)*

MICHELLE HIRAISHI *(above)*

What I love the most about *Stranger Things* is how it's the type of show that brings friends, family, and other people together. As the season is airing, everyone at work always asks, "Did you watch *Stranger Things*? What did you think of the episode? Or about such-and-such character?" It blends together so many unique aspects of horror, comedy, and heartwarming moments that people are so moved, they cannot wait to discuss it.

MICHELLE PREBICH
It's pretty amazing, the pop culture phenomenon that *Stranger Things* has become. I feel it taps into this nostalgia zeitgeist: People are currently yearning for a time before technology dominated our attention spans and back pockets. Also, I never thought I'd ever hear a Clash song juxtaposed with horror! Thank you, *Stranger Things,* for being bitchin'.

RAFAL ROLA (right)

STEPHANIE ROSALES (right)

Stranger Things had me hooked in the very first ten minutes of Season 1, when Mike, Dustin, Lucas, and Will play Dungeons & Dragons. When I was their age, *that* was my group—the outsider nerd kids, heavy into fantasy.

That age is also a very memorable time—kids feel that their parents are out of touch with them and what they're going through, that friends are the only ones who understand their struggles; crushes or first loves impact and change our lives; and, maybe for the first time, we're aware of how willing we are to put others before us. It's a rainbow of emotions. Love, loss, pain, longing, hope, and happiness are relatable to everyone. Also, I'm getting to relive my teenage years (minus Demogorgons) through the characters. That's what brings me back for more.

LIZA SHUMSKAYA *(left)*

JONNY WELLMAN *(below)*

STRANGER THINGS

HAWKINS NATIONAL LABORATORY
U.S. DEPARTMENT OF ENERGY

Project MKUltra (CIA mind control program)
Subject No.11 is to be placed in a sensory deprivation tank
where she can engage in astral projection and access other dimensions.
Studies will be conducted using septal electrodes, and investigations
will be managed on the geography of the brain to develop her psychokinetic skills.
[Clasified] Office of Scientific Intelligence.

011
Eleven (Jane Ives)
Hawkins, Indiana, 1983.

JOHN SLOBODA *(left)*

Stranger Things captures so much for my age group; having been a kid myself during the time of most of the action, the homages, references, and "Easter eggs" feel tailor-made for me. We loved the same stuff. I still love that stuff! And the fact that the main characters are all kids themselves only elevates that emotional connection. Even the score to this show is an homage to those John Carpenter/Alan Howarth pieces that were so integral to that perfect blend of sci-fi, horror, and suspense. I love Eleven. I love Dustin . . . I could go on and on—but needless to say, I'm hooked!

RANDY SIPLON

MATT BUSCH (above)

STELLA LEE-HSU (right)
Ice Cream brings such joy
Sorry friends: fend for yourselves
El just needs a break

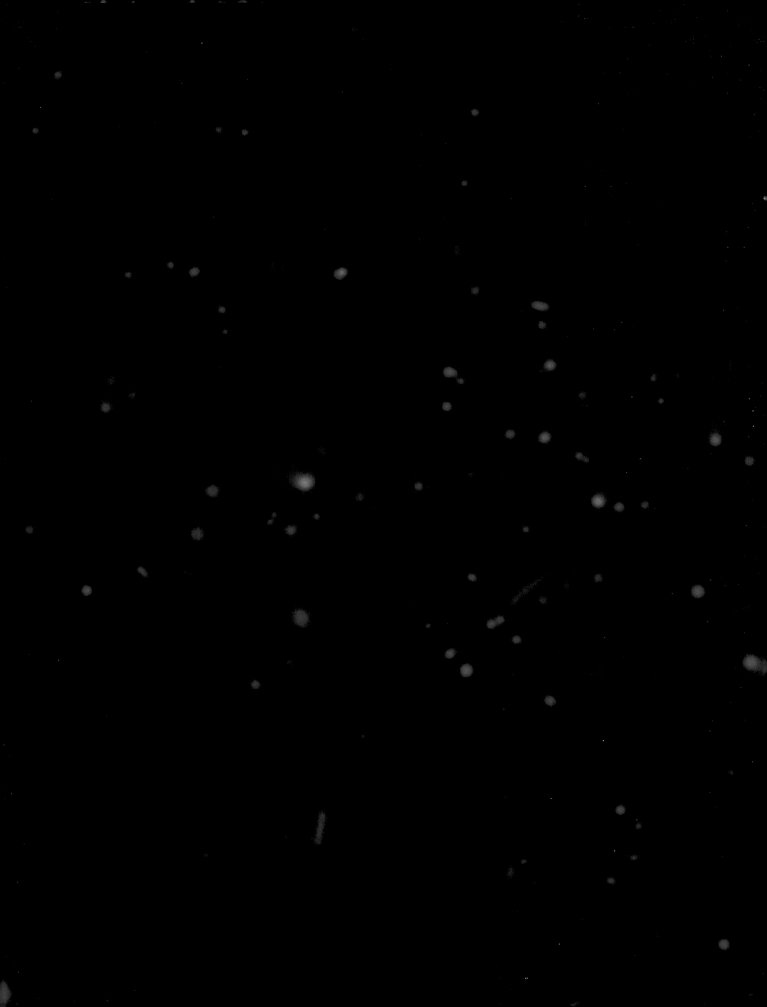

BUSCH, MATT - 18, 127, 128, 188, 234
@matt_busch_instagram

BUTCHER BILLY - 66
@thebutcherbilly

C., SHEILA - 216
@studiosheila

CABALEIRO, CARLOS - 142
@cabaleiroart

CALLAHAN, CHRIS - 208
@rgb_alpha

CAMPBELL, JOSH - 49
@paybackpenguin

CAMPOS, DANIEL - 78
@stalk_danielcampos

CARLETON, KATE - 70
@keelhaulkate

CARPENTER, SIMON - 190
@simcarpe

CASKEY, RYAN - 192
@ryancaskeyillustration

CASSANO, CHRISTA - 186
@christacassano

CASTANEDA, JUSTIN - 193
@whenuwerelittle

CASTRO, VICTOR - 219
@victoroil

CHAN, LON - 218
@lonchanillustrates

CHEREPANOV, ALEXANDER - 35
@cherepanov_inkart

CHOGRIN - 169
@chogrin

CHOMICHUK, GMB - 80
@gmbchomichuk

CHUCKRY, CHRISTOPHER - 33
@chrischuckry

COBURN-JAMES, DARREN - 148
@asylumartz

COCKERTON, ADAM - 83
@adamcockertonart

CORRONEY, JOE - 191
@joecorroney

CRAGGS, CAROLYN - 144
@carriejc1983

CREMIN, PAUL - 101
@paul_cremin_art

CROSBY, RYAN - 92
@rcillustration

CROWTHER, RONNIE - 55
@ronniecrowtherart

CUNNIFFE, DEE - 24
@deezoid

CURIOUS ART GLASS - 174
@curiousartglass

CURRIE, JUSTIN - 211
@chasingartwork

DAHLSTROM, BOB - 58
@bobdahlstrom

DASTICK, TED - 30
@teddastickjr (Twitter)

DAVIES, JASON - 69
@jasondaviesart_

DAVIES, NEIL - 54
@neildaviesillustration1

DAVIES, RICH - 8
@turksworks

DELART, SIMON - 126
@s2lart

DIAZ, MIGUEL (MIKE) - 112

DIX, GARRETT - 63
@garrett_dix_artist

DOLLAH, RODNEY - 102
@rodneydollah

DUG NATION - 160
@sketchymonsters

DUNN, MATTHEW - 40
@matthewdunnart

DUQUE, ROBERTO - 71
@rad_pencils

EDWARDSON, DAMIAN - 62
@damianedwardsonart

ELKINS, SARAH - 215
@NeilaK20 (Twitter)

ENGLAND, DON - 39
@donaldengland_art

FALK, NICOLE - 222—223
@legendsofthefalk

FAULK, BASTIAN - 166
@bastianfaulk

FILER, JAIMIE - 52
@jaimie_filer

FISHER, MALCOLM - 163
@mal_made

FLORES, FRANCISCO - 165
@artofmetalhand

FLORES, JARED (CIRCUSBEAR) - 104
@jaredcircusbear

FORDHAM, JULIE - 197
@juliefordham

FRANCIS, LUKE - 99
@twistedabnormality

FRANCISCO, DEVIN - 17
@devin_francisco_art

FYFFE, BRYAN - 187
@bryanfyffe

GALATIS, ANTHONY - 124
@anthonygalatis

GATES, PAUL - 34
@pickle.vision -

GERLACH, BRUCE - 36
@bruce_gerlach *(Twitter)*

GILBEY, SAM - 143
@samgilbey

GILLIES, DONNY - 87
@dirtydonnyart

GOEBEL, DUSTIN - 196
@dgoebel00

GOUNGOR, JASON - 103
@jasongoungor

GRAFUNKEL, ART - 41, 146
@artgrafunkel

GREEN, JOSHUA - 201
@lvciferx

HANARO, ANWAR - 219

HARDER, JUSTIN - 79
@clausstudios

HARRISON-DAVIES, PAUL - 132
@paulmhd

HARROWER, MATTHEW - 42
@hpmatt1984

HART, JORDAN - 93
@jordyjordith

HEARD, SIMON - 133
@sinagedesign

HIJO, TOMAS - 175
@tomashijo

HILL, JOHN J. - 158
@johnjhill

HIRAISHI, MICHELLE - 225
@_mhiraishi

HIRONS, MATTHEW - 167
@saintworksart

HITCHMAN, CHRIS - 19
@chris_hitchman

HOBSON, JAMES - 224
@jamesjamesjamescreative

HODGKINSON, TONY - 60
@epictonedogg

HOWARD, JOSH - 220
@josh_howard

HUGHES, FARYN - 28
@farynh

HUGHES, RIAN - 168
@rianhughes

HUNT, JON - 107, 153
@huntillustration

JEPSON, IAN - 98
@ian_jepson

JEZOWSKI, BERNIE - 199
@berniedave

JIMENEZ, ROBERT - 200
@zerostreet

JOEJR - 221
@joejrberrelleza

KAAN, ADEM - 65
@ademkaanillustration

KAHANA, ANA - 204
@kahanita

KAMENZ, SANDRA - 88, 176
@sandrakamenz

KAY, CHRIS - 141
@chris_kay_art

KELLEHER, MICHAEL - 47
@michaelkelleherillustrator *(Facebook)*

KELLY, JOSH - 159
@jmonsterart

KELLY, TOM 43
@tomkellyart

KLEIN, JEMMA - 59
@jemmaklein

LANDRY, HEATHER - 205
@sandpaperdaisy

LAROCCA, DOUG - 137
@douglaroccaart

LEE-HSU, STELLA - 235

LEVY, MARK - 85
@marklevyart

LI, ALICE MEICHI - 189
@alicemeichi

LINEHAM, MATTHEW - 129
@mlinehamart

LOWE, CHELSEA - 51
@cmloweart

MA, JERRY - 89
@epicprops

MacDOUGALL, IAN - 202
@ianmacart

MAHLE, MIKE - 14
@mikemahleart

MAJEWSKI, TOMASZ - 203
@tomasz.majewski

MALBON, CHRIS - 156
@melbs74

MANLOVE, MATT - 16
@mattmanlove

MAUL, CHRISTOPHER - 76
@christopher_maul

MAYLE, SAM - 108
@sammaylearts

McCLANAHAN, KRISTOPHER - 207
@deeplydapper

McCONKEY, BILL - 9
@bill_mcconkey

McCREA, JOHN - 24
@mccreaman1

McKAY, SCOTT - 21
@thescottmckay

MEDELLIN, AXEL - 15
@axelmedellinmachain

MIGLIORI, KELLY - 77
@heyghoulhey

MILLER, JASON - 138
@jasonmillerart

MOMOKO, PEACH - 20
@peachmomoko60

MORINISHI, AKANE - 86
@akaneschibiart

MURUGIAH - 106
@_murugiah

NANNIPIERI, CHRISTIAN - 48
@christian.nannipieri

NEEDLE, MATT - 23
@needledesign

NOS4A2 DESIGN - 152
@nos4a2lives

O'NEILL, WILLIAM - 10
@william.oneill.792

ONOFRE, ANGEL - 154
@angelonofre

PAEZ, REYNALDO - 131
@reypaezart

PARKER, LUKE - 206
@artofparker

PEARSON, JOHN - 13
@johnjpearson

PENALTA, XURXO - 125
@xurxogpenalta

ESCE, JERRY - 209
@pesceffects

ESTMEESTER - 110
@thepestmeester

EVERILL, LUCAS - 68
@lucas_peverill (Twitter)

REBICH, MICHELLE - 226
@batinyourbelfry

RYOR, DAVE - 130
@davepryor72

ULLIN, GARY - 122
@ghoulishgary

QUEEN, L. JASON - 64, 210
@ljasonqueen

EQUENA, ALDO - 117
@aldorequenavalgorth

EX, JOEY - 198
@iamjoeyrex

EYES, RODOLFO - 50
@rodolforever

RICO, ALEKSEY - 212
@alekseyrico

ICO JR, JULIEN - 149
@julienricojr

ILEY, DYLAN - 140
@dylandraw

ISTE, MATT - 111
@mattristeillustration

OLA, RAFAL - 227
@rolarafal

OSALES, STEPHANIE - 229
@rosalesart1 (Twitter)

AMPSON, STEPHEN "DARKINKER"- 44
@thedarkinker

ASLOW, SCOTT - 94
@scottsaslow

AVARIE, VALERIE - 105
@valeriesavarie

CAR STUDIO - 116
@antoinette.rydyr (Facebook)

CHNEIDER, JAMES "BOARDINKER" DORMER - 38
@boardinker

HADOWS, MARKEE - 147
@markeeshadows

HARPSTEN, TAYLOR - 219

HIRTS, JERRY - 228
@artisticaerosol

HUMSKAYA, LIZA - 230
@kino_maniac

SIENKIEWICZ, BILL - 82
@therealthatpolishguy

SIPLON, RANDY - 233
@randysiplon

SLOBODA, JOHN - 232
@sloboart

SORIANO, BRIAN - 53
@wrathcomics

STANLEY, ROB - 120
@robstanleyart

STAUBER, GUY - 12
@guystauber

STEINBACH, EILEEN - 25
@sg_posters

STEVENSON, BLAKE - 37
@jetpacksandrollerskates

STEWART, JUSTIN - 121
@justin3000stewart

STEWART, MATT - 151
@stewartillustrations

STEWART, R. H. - 170
@rhsillustratorgmailcom

STONE, GLEN - 29
@glenstoneillustration

STOTHARD, ADAM - 46
@ad_illustrator

STREIT, LAURA - 150
@laurastreit_art

STROUD, MARK - 194
@markstroud81

SWAINSON, ANDREW - 84
@andrew_swainson

TAYLOR, NICK - 91
@nickillustratesthings

THEORETICAL PART - 171
@theoreticalpart

THOMAS, STEVE - 173
@stevethomasart

TIERNAN, KEVIN - 172
@jurassickevin

TINDALL, FELIX - 177
@f_tindall

TRANCON, ANGEL - 118, 119
@angeltranconstudio

TULLY, WAYNE - 114
@waynetully

VROSH, CODY - 195
@codyvrosh

WELLMAN, JONNY - 231
@jonnys_pixels

WEST, BRYAN - 73
@bryanwestart

WESTBROOK, TRENT BRIAN - 113
@2023comics

WILLDIG, CHRIS - 90
@rebelart1984

WOODS, MATTHEW - 136
@hallowwoods

WOOLSTON, SCOTT - 214
@scottwool

YEAGER, CLINTON - 115
@screamingclint

Social media accounts are all
INSTAGRAM unless noted otherwise.

SPECIAL THANKS

The Printed In Blood team would like to thank the following fine people:
KIM LAWRENCE, TARA SINCLAIR and the entire NETFLIX licensing team,
ELIZABETH SCHAEFER, KEITH CLAYTON and the entire P/RH team, ROSS
and MATT DUFFER, MADISON, DLBROOKS, RYANE LYNN HILL, PHOEBE
and RIPLEY. Without them, you'd be holding an entirely different book.

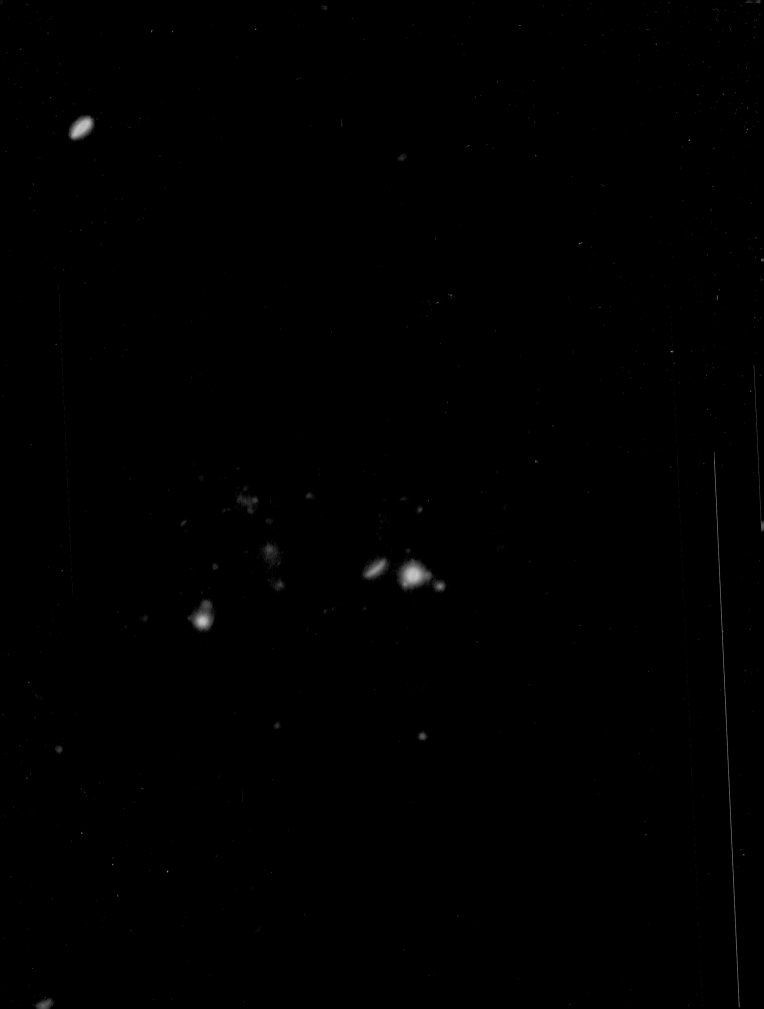